BRITISH VALUES AND THE PREVENT DUTY IN THE EARLY YEARS

of related interest

Positive Behaviour Management in Early Years Settings
An Essential Guide
Liz Williams
ISBN 978 1 78592 026 4
eISBN 978 1 78450 273 7

Equipping Young People to Choose Non-Violence
A Violence Reduction Programme to Understand Violence,
Its Effects, Where It Comes From and How to Prevent It
Gerry Heery
ISBN 978 1 84905 265 8
eISBN 978 0 85700 605 9

Young Children and Racial Justice
Taking action for racial equality in the early years – understanding
the past, thinking about the present, planning for the future
Jane Lane
Foreword by Herman Ousley
ISBN 978 1 90581 825 9
eISBN 978 1 90581 887 7

BRITISH VALUES
—— AND THE ——
PREVENT DUTY IN THE EARLY YEARS
A PRACTITIONER'S GUIDE

Kerry Maddock

Jessica Kingsley *Publishers*
London and Philadelphia

First published in 2017
by Jessica Kingsley Publishers
73 Collier Street
London N1 9BE, UK
and
400 Market Street, Suite 400
Philadelphia, PA 19106, USA

www.jkp.com

Library of Congress Cataloging in Publication Data
Names: Maddock, Kerry, author.
Title: British values and the Prevent duty in the early years : a
    practitioner's guide / Kerry Maddock.
Description: London : Jessica Kingsley Publishers, 2017.
Identifiers: LCCN 2016041274 | ISBN 9781785920486 (alk. paper)
Subjects: LCSH: Moral education (Early childhood)--Great Britain. |
    Values--Study and teaching (Early childhood)--Great Britain.
Classification: LCC LB1139.35.M67 M33 2017 | DDC 370.11/40941-
-dc23 LC record available at https://lccn.loc.gov/2016041274

British Library Cataloguing in Publication Data
A CIP catalogue record for this book is available from the British Library.

ISBN 978 1 78592 048 6
eISBN 978 1 78450 307 9

Printed and bound in Great Britain

CONTENTS

ACKNOWLEDGEMENTS

I would like to thank the people who contributed to the production of this book. To Sue Miller[1] who was fantastic in every way. Thank you also to Neil Blumsom and Linda Jones for their contributions and to the Early Years' settings who have graciously shared their practice and completed questionnaires. A very big thank you to Eric Cohen (otherwise known as 'the Jewish fellow') who supported me throughout the conception of the book.

Thank you also to my wonderful family and the exceptional team at my nursery, without whom this book would not have been possible.

---

1   You can visit Sue's website at www.allwordsmatter.co.uk.

INTRODUCTION

As practitioners, it is vital that we understand the recent changes in legislation, best practice and expectations that have taken place since the introduction of the Prevent Duty and the common inspection framework. It is important also that we understand how to integrate these changes into our settings and our everyday practice.

In this book we will explore the meaning of:

- Democracy

- Rule of Law

- Individual Liberty

- Mutual Respect and Tolerance

We will also explore how to evidence this through our daily practice and planning.

We will look in depth at the Prevent Duty and how this affects our policies, procedures and relationships with staff, children and families. We will also hear the views and opinions of Early Years' settings and childminders, Early Years' lecturers and local authority advisors.

The idea that we as a British nation have a set of values and ethics that should be adhered to is not a new idea. However, if we asked someone 100, 50 or even 10 years ago what those values were, they would probably be very different to the ones that have been outlined by the government today.

Initially there was limited guidance that explained to the Early Years' sector what the introduction of British values would mean in practice. As a result, many practitioners and settings would celebrate 'Fish and Chip Fridays' or plan to have tea with the Queen, without fully realising the underlying message of inclusion and support for all members of society. As time has passed, more practitioners are realising that British values are about kindness, acceptance and respect, while still giving us the opportunity to celebrate who we are as individuals, settings and communities within our nation, and whilst celebrating being part of a global community.

'British values' is a term that we in the Early Years have been dealing with since 2014, but what *are* British values? Why have they been introduced now? How do these values affect us as practitioners? What will be the impact upon the children we teach? This book will explore what effective practice looks like in Early Years' settings across the country. We will look at policy and procedure, the environment and the 'Prevent Duty'.

WHERE DID IT ALL START?

In March 2014, Birmingham City Council revealed it was investigating a number of Muslim schools following a letter suggesting that there was a plot within these schools to install school governors who were sympathetic to teaching a strong Islamist or Salafist-based curriculum and ethos. The letter claimed that head teachers had been pushed from their posts, and teachers who were not sympathetic were marginalised.

The announcement came after pressure from head teachers, police and the Department for Education following claims that senior council officials had been aware of the allegations for some time, indeed well before the 'Trojan Horse' letter was received, and no formal attempt had been made to investigate the original complaint.

The 'Trojan Horse' letter referred to a document that was allegedly sent to an unnamed person in Bradford detailing how Tahir Alam, a well-known figure in education circles in Birmingham, had 'fine-tuned the "Trojan Horse" [operation] so that it is totally invisible to the naked eye and allows us to operate under the radar'.

It then goes on to describe a five-stage process to remove head teachers and take control of schools:

- Identify your schools.

- Select a group of Salafi parents.

- Put our own governor in.

- Identify key staff to disrupt the school from within.

- Create an anonymous letter and PR campaign.

The letter concludes that 'all these things will work towards wearing the Head down, removing his/her resolve and weakening their mind-set so they eventually just give up'.

In light of these concerns and reports from both the Office for Standards in Education, Children's Services and Skills (Ofsted) and the Department of Education, the House of Commons ordered an investigation into how this type of activity was allowed to go unchallenged. The report published in July 2014 made 15 recommendations including the recommendation for Ofsted to revise the then-current inspection framework to incorporate identification of early indicators of extremism.

Although the introduction of British values came as a result of activities within one sector of the community, we must be open-minded to all cultures which face ongoing challenges with integration in to a multi-cultural society.

The recommendations from this report were the basis of the changes to the Early Years Foundation Stage (EYFS) framework and inspection systems that we have in place today.

All pages marked with the ✳ symbol can be accessed at www.jkp.com/voucher using the code MADDOCKVALUES to be printed and used with the book.

CHAPTER 1

BRITISH VALUES

The Early Years Foundations Stage framework has always provided statutory guidance for settings and practitioners. The introduction of British values fits within this template under the headings of Personal, Social and Emotional Development and Understanding of the World. Ofsted inspects British values under these headings and base their judgements on how well the four themes of **Democracy**, **Rule of Law**, **Individual Liberty** and **Mutual Respect and Tolerance** are embedded within practice. Here, we will break down what each theme means to practitioners and the children for whom we care.

DEMOCRACY

Democracy by definition means governance by the people. In the United Kingdom, we live in a democratic society; we take for granted our right to vote for the party that will, in our opinion, be the best to govern our country for a set period of time based upon a manifesto of ideas and promises. We understand that just because we voted for our chosen party, it doesn't mean that they will necessarily win the election, as all votes have to be taken into account and the majority wins. We are able to understand this as we have learned about the process through schools, experienced our grandparents and parents voting and, finally, being able to vote ourselves once we turn 18 years of age. Through this process, we are empowered with the knowledge that our vote counts, that our opinion matters and we are, to some extent, part of the decision-making process.

When we involve the children democratically in their learning through asking for ideas, thoughts and suggestions, the children begin to feel valued, included and part of their own decision making.

As practitioners, sometimes it is too easy to plan a day, activity or interest focus without involving the children. We assume because we have spent hours on Pinterest looking for the perfect activity and carefully planned our goals to meet every child's next steps, that the children will be as excited about it as we are. But, without asking them or involving them in the planning process, we will only really know how interested they are once the activity has finished. This approach is almost like putting the cart before the horse! We need to reverse our thinking and start with the children: their likes, dislikes, interests and abilities. We can ask and value their input before we start to plan. When children are involved in their learning, they are excited to participate and willing to learn.

Including the children's input

Below are some of the ways in which including the children's input can be done effectively.

Planning

Children can be involved in the planning process of the setting and can provide a unique insight into medium- and short-term plans. Often, when we ask the children what they would like to do they come up with ideas that we hadn't thought of.

Daily and weekly planning provide optimum opportunities for children to experience the outcomes of their input. Planning too far in advance is not as effective, as children's capacity to understand time is limited.

Opportunities to vote

There are many opportunities for us to give our children the chance to vote. We do not have to create a ballot box and have secret votes; a simple show of hands is a good place to start. Outings, trips, activities and continuous provision-area enhancements (literacy, maths, messy play and so forth) are just some of the ways to demonstrate a true democratic setting.

Consider next how to include and value the voices of other stakeholders such as parents/carers and extended families. Gone are the days where sending out a questionnaire before parents' evening was enough to prove active involvement.

Termly direction meetings

Direction meetings at the start of each term are one way to involve parents in the self-evaluation and forward planning of the setting. Parents are invited to attend a meeting with managers and staff to discuss as a combined unit the current strengths, areas for development and the challenges facing the nursery in an informal environment.

Questionnaires

Questionnaires still have their place, but they have to be meaningful, honest and you must be willing to act on the feedback you receive. Different types of questionnaires serve different purposes. A formal questionnaire may be handed out at parents' evening on a termly basis, while an informal questionnaire could be used to ask what information sessions parents would benefit from that term or ask for a suggestion of the month.

Boards: 'you said/we did'

When you are open to receiving information, people will feel more comfortable sharing their thoughts and views. If you ask the questions but do not act upon the feedback, people will stop answering the questions. One way to demonstrate you are listening to your families is to create a 'you said/we did' board. The board has to be updated and/or changed regularly to keep parents interested and involved. For example, one month you ask a question of the quality of your menus and what parents would like to see more or less of. The following month, when all the suggestions have been gathered, you can clearly show the percentage of respondents who are very happy, satisfied, neutral, not happy and how you have adapted your menus by displaying the old menu and a new menu based on their feedback. You can also show how the children are reacting to their new foods.

Family outings

Once a term, invite your parents on a family trip. Ask parents where they would like to go and to make suggestions for the next outing. Try to ensure that the place that is chosen is one that is accessible to all families. Consider transport links for those who don't drive, cost for those on limited budgets and/or large families and how it will support children of different age groups.

Social media

There is a huge rise in the number of people using social media, and for busy families it provides a way of contact and information sharing at a time that is convenient to them. For settings, it provides a way to share information, events, good practice, photographs from the day and anecdotes to a large number of people quickly and easily.

RULE OF LAW

Every country has their own laws that must be abided by. The laws are created to keep the people safe from harm and to maintain order in society. Rules in settings are no different; we expect children to follow rules that are designed to keep them and others safe. We need to support the understanding that individual behaviour affects others and that actions have consequences.

In order for children to follow rules, they must first understand what the rules are. Often we expect children to behave a certain way because of our own ideas and prejudices on what we deem to be acceptable or unacceptable behaviour. A more effective approach would be to define a set of expectations which has been discussed and agreed upon by management, staff and children.

The revised EYFS 2014 removed the requirement for a named behaviour management coordinator. This places responsibility on all staff as individuals to support and promote positive behaviour throughout the setting. The aim of this approach was to ensure that staff were able to deal with behaviours, both positive and negative, in an effective way.

Every setting will have their own ideas on how positive behaviour should be supported and how unacceptable behaviour is managed. For example, some settings will find it appropriate to use a 'time out' or 'reflection time', while other settings will feel that if positive behaviour is supported effectively, there will be no need for such strategies. There is no handbook or statutory guidance stating exactly what your behaviour management should look like, except for the guidance that is given under section 3.52 of the EYFS statutory guidance which states:

3.52. Providers are responsible for managing children's behaviour in an appropriate way. Providers must not give corporal punishment to a child. Providers must take all reasonable steps to ensure that corporal punishment is not given by any person who cares for or is in regular contact with a child, or by any person living or working in the premises where care is provided. Any early years' provider who fails to meet these requirements commits an offence. A person will not be taken to have used corporal punishment (and therefore will not have committed an offence), where physical intervention was taken for the purposes of averting immediate danger of personal injury to any person (including the child) or to manage a child's behaviour if absolutely necessary. Providers, including childminders, must keep a record of any occasion where physical intervention is used, and parents and/or carers must be informed on the same day, or as soon as reasonably practicable.

3.53. Providers must not threaten corporal punishment, and must not use or threaten any punishment which could adversely affect a child's well-being.

Embedding Rule of Law in practice

When you consider how the Rule of Law is already embedded within your practice, I am certain that you will find lots of good practice. Below are some good-practice examples for you to consider.

Policy and procedures

Having a clear, well-defined policy that is implemented in a consistent manner by all staff is the foundation stone for good practice. It is important that parents/carers and families be aware of policies to ensure consistency for the children. (We will look in depth at policy and procedure in Chapter 2.)

Child involvement

Children need to understand what is expected of them in terms of behaviour. One way of building on this is to allow the children to create the rules themselves. Ask them what is good behaviour and which behaviours they don't like. Allow the children to create a display for their golden rules, whether it be a board or a poster at their height. This will encourage children to remind themselves and others of what is expected.

Parental involvement

Sometimes there can be a difference in expectations between home and nursery. This is not uncommon; however, these differences are not always known until an incident occurs. When nursery expectations are made clear in pre-registration materials, such as on the website and in the prospectus, parents have a chance to ask questions on practice and make an informed decision about whether this is the right setting for their child.

INDIVIDUAL LIBERTY: FREEDOM FOR ALL

Liberty is defined as the freedom not to be constrained by another person's will, with the exception that one's will does not harm another. It doesn't mean that we can do whatever we like whenever we want. Individual liberty cannot have adverse effects on the wider group. Nursery life would become quite complicated if every child was able to access the entire continuous provision at all times without structure. We have a duty to meet the needs of the group as a whole and to ensure that when the children leave us that, as an individual, they are 'school ready'.

To help us create a balance that fosters Individual Liberty and conformity, we create routines that provide us with a structure for the day with elements of flexible planning. For example, circle/welcome time: we could tell the same story and sing the same songs and expect children to comply, or we could ask the children to be involved in a show-and-tell activity which would allow them the freedom to share something from home with the group and build upon their self-confidence.

As a sector, we are very good at adapting activities and areas to follow children's needs and interests, *but* we do have a tendency to restrict children's freedom in the name of health and safety.

We can become overprotective by restricting types of play and risk-taking in the name of keeping children safe. Does it take a brave setting to allow the use of real hammers and nails or one that will support the child through their learning process and allow them to judge the risk for themselves?

Freedom of speech

We are all entitled to our opinions and are equally entitled to express those opinions again provided they do not hurt another person. This is firmly rooted in the Prevent Duty which we explore more in Chapter 4.

In settings, we need to promote the idea that children have a right to an opinion and that it is okay for someone else to have an opinion that is different. It is the ability to challenge or accept these differences that enables us to remain free and respectful. It is by allowing children to explore freely their likes, dislikes, similarities and differences that they create a positive sense of self-building, self-confidence and self-awareness.

Allowing children to make their own choices is a key element to promoting Individual Liberty. A supportive key-person approach encourages children to explore the risks and challenges within the environment in a safe way while allowing them the time to consider the consequences of their actions.

MUTUAL RESPECT AND TOLERANCE

In essence, mutual respect is treating others as you wish to be treated. Tolerance generally means being open-minded without prejudice to the views and beliefs of others. While it is important that Mutual Respect and Tolerance relates to every person regardless of ethnicity, beliefs or religion, we find these values becoming increasingly important as diversity grows.

In the year ending September 2015, immigration to the United Kingdom stood at 617,000. The most culturally diverse cities in 2015 were London and its surrounding boroughs, Leicester, Slough, Luton and Birmingham. With the number of immigrants entering Britain increasing, we find ourselves rapidly learning about other cultures from other cultures and adapting our settings to be even more inclusive.

Early Years' settings have a legal duty to meet the requirements set out in the Equality Act 2010 and a moral duty to welcome families of all cultural backgrounds. It is our aim to create a culture of inclusivity, an environment that is welcoming and a curriculum that supports a meaningful understanding of the world today.

Within areas of greater diversity, it is easier to create this culture of inclusivity as settings are able to draw on the knowledge and expertise of the local community. Areas that are less diverse must look further afield to make the wider community come to them if they are not to create a tokenistic environment.

Local places of worship such as churches, mosques, synagogues and gurdwaras are a fantastic place to start and are open to sharing information about their beliefs and the community that they support. Other community, private or voluntary groups can be found on the Internet or in the local paper and again are almost always willing to share their experiences with young children.

It is important that we not forget our own culture in the exploration of others. We must celebrate what makes Britain great – our local and national history – and what it means to be British.

Celebrations of all cultures must be meaningful and provide an opportunity for all children to explore other cultures. Food, clothing, stories, dance and music are all interactive ways to bring celebrations to life. Involving parents in celebrations is also a vital part of our teaching. By educating the whole family, we enable knowledge and remove ignorance, breaking down barriers to prejudice.

There are those who disagree with these values or challenge that they are the correct values to represent 'Britishness'; however, these are the definitions that we have been given by the government to provide us with a stepping stone on which to build and reflect.

CHAPTER 2

POLICIES AND PROCEDURES

Good policies and procedures are the foundation stones of Early Years' settings. They provide clear expectations and a framework that ensures high-quality practice is followed by everyone involved with the setting.

There is no requirement to have separate policies for either British values or Prevent Duty; however, by ensuring quality policies and procedures, we can demonstrate our commitment to both.

The table that follows highlights some key policies and gives points to consider when reviewing your documentation. Creating a set of policies that reflects your ethos, vision and daily practice is an important part of making your setting unique and sets you apart from other Early Years' settings.

You can access a template to print and document your current policies and the action you need to take to improve at www.jkp.com/voucher using the code MADDOCKVALUES.

Policy	Points to Consider
EAL (English as an Additional Language)	How well do you support EAL in your setting?
	Have any staff completed training on EAL? Is this shown in your policy?
	How well do you support parents and families with EAL?
	How do you document community involvement and support?
	Do you employ the services of a translator for parental involvement, for example parents' evening or newsletters?
	Do you have key phrases simplified in multiple languages that you could use in an emergency to contact parents such as 'nursery name – child's name – illness – please come to collect'?
	Are you involved with support services through the local authority?
Safeguarding and Child Protection	Does your policy cover female genital mutilation exploitation including arranged marriages and Internet threats such as cyber-bullying, grooming and the risk of exposure to extremist ideology?
	Do you have a clear statement on your commitment to train staff in all aspects of safeguarding including the Prevent Duty?
	Do you have a written risk assessment detailing: • population • levels of employment • access to services • community services and dynamics including local groups?
	Do you have a risk assessment taking into consideration community dynamics?

Inclusion and Equality	Are fundamental British values demonstrated throughout the policy?
Discriminatory Behaviour	Does your policy make clear that you support fundamental British values and that any discriminatory behaviour will not be tolerated by children, staff and families?
	Are the nine protected characteristics of • age • disability • race • sex • gender reassignment • sexual orientation • pregnancy and maternity • religion and belief • marriage or civil partnership evidenced throughout the policy?
Promoting Positive Behaviour	How are children supported to resolve conflict for themselves?
	Do all staff respond to behaviour in the same way regardless of personal opinions?
Visits and Outings	Is a wide range of places from different cultures visited?
	Do you have regular visits to your setting from local community and cultural groups?
	Do your visits and outings cover local places of interest and promote local history and culture?

Policy	Points to Consider
Healthy Workplace	Do you have procedures in place to support staff's morale, cultural and religious needs?
	How do you support staff well-being? Are all staff aware of the procedures and support you have in place?
	How is the emotional health of the staff promoted?
	Do you ask during supervision and appraisal how routines, rotas and duties may be adapted to improve the quality of the working environment and structure?
	How do you support a healthy work-life balance for all staff?
Critical Incident	Do you have clear procedures in place for the safety and evacuation of children, staff and members of the public should there be an attack or threat of an attack on or near your setting?
	Do you have contingency plans if your setting is unable to be used for any period of time?
Early Learning Opportunities/ Curriculum Development	Do you clearly set out how you will actively promote fundamental British values?
	Do you demonstrate how all seven areas of learning will be covered in daily practice and routines?
	Are parents and children actively involved in the planning of opportunities that support learning and development?
Nutrition and Mealtimes	Do you provide dietary choices to meet different cultures and preferences, including: • vegetarian • vegan • halal • kosher? Are choices available for parents/carers to view?

Conflict with Parents (challenging behaviour)	Are parents aware that views that are contradictory to British values will not be tolerated?
	Do parents feel that their views, opinions and choices are valued in a positive way?
Parents and Carers as Partners	How do you support parents in their understanding of the seven areas of learning including how you promote local, national and international celebrations?
	How do you keep parents informed of visitors coming in and their purpose?
	How do you inform parents and carers how to make their views known both in person and anonymously?
	Can parents see how their views and suggestions make a difference to the setting?
Admission Policy	Do you ask parents if they have any skills, talents, or professional or cultural knowledge they can share with the setting?
	Do you ask for primary and secondary languages for parents and children?
	Can parents include religious, cultural and dietary requirements?
Recruitment and Selection	Does your policy demonstrate how your setting is inclusive for people of all backgrounds, ethnicity, religions and cultures?
	How do you evaluate and monitor the recruitment process to prove that it is non-discriminatory?
	Do you allow religious holidays to be taken on their set days either as paid or unpaid leave?
	Do you have contingencies for staff who may not be able to work set days or times for religious or cultural requirements?

Policy	Points to Consider
E-safety, Mobile Phone and Social Networking	Do your policies clearly demonstrate an awareness of potential risks associated with the use of the Internet to access inappropriate content online?
	Does it state how you will keep children and staff from accessing inappropriate materials through the use of firewalls and restrictions?
	Do you allow staff to use setting's Wi-Fi to access the Internet? If so, does your policy clearly state that firewalls are in place to restrict the ability to access inappropriate materials?
	Is it clear that viewing or attempting to view inappropriate materials may result in disciplinary actions?
	Are staff shown from induction that mobile phones are not permitted in areas where children are present?
	Do staff sign mobile phones in and out at the start of the day and during break periods?
	Do you periodically check the content of phones for Internet usage and pictures? Are staff aware of this?
	Do staff keep their social networking settings to private?
	Does your policy allow staff to befriend parents/ families of children? If so, are there clear expectations of professionalism?
Absence Management Procedure	Do you have effective systems in place to monitor child absence?
	Are there clear reporting systems to inform safeguarding boards and local authority where child absence is regular or unexplained?

CHAPTER 3

PERSONAL, SOCIAL AND EMOTIONAL DEVELOPMENT

Personal, social and emotional development is a vital part of how we learn to interact with others, how we decode our own feelings and how we learn to manage our own expectations and the expectations of others. Personal, social and emotional development is broken down into the following three subheadings: making relationships; self-confidence and awareness; and managing feelings and behaviour. In this chapter we will look at ways to promote fundamental British values through supporting children's personal, social and emotional development.

You can access templates of the tables that follow to print at www.jkp.com/voucher using the code MADDOCKVALUES.

MAKING RELATIONSHIPS

This table explores personal, social and emotional development in the context of making relationships.

Age Group	EYFS Learning Outcomes	Activities and Ideas for Best Practice

Birth to 26 months	• Enjoys the company of others and seeks contact with others from birth
	• Gazes at faces and copies facial movements (e.g. sticking out tongue, opening mouth and widening eyes)
	• Responds when talked to (e.g. moves arms and legs, changes facial expression, moves body and makes mouth movements)
	• Recognises and is most responsive to main carer's voice: face brightens, activity increases when familiar carer appears
	• Responds to what carer is paying attention to (e.g. following their gaze)
	• Likes cuddles and being held: calms, snuggles in, smiles, gazes at carer's face or strokes carer's skin
	• Seeks to gain attention in a variety of ways, drawing others into social interaction
	• Builds relationships with special people
	  • Is wary of unfamiliar people
	  • Interacts with others and explores new situations when supported by familiar person
		The key-person system allows children, families and settings to build relationships based on trust and respect. An effective system will gather information before the child starts so that routines, likes, dislikes and methods of communication are all understood and used to make the transition process as smooth as possible.
		
		Babies and young children learn to recognise the voice and faces of people who are familiar to them, so promoting songs, stories and action rhymes is important in daily routines.
		
		Relationships between children build over time in small groups. Ensuring that these group times are spent with meaningful activities and opportunities to communicate and explore will encourage the children to join in.

	• Shows interest in the activities of others and responds differently to children and adults (e.g. may be more interested in watching children than adults or may pay more attention when children talk to them) • Plays alongside others • Uses a familiar adult as a secure base from which to explore independently in new environments (e.g. ventures away to play and interact with others, but returns for a cuddle or reassurance if becomes anxious) • Plays cooperatively with a familiar adult (e.g. rolling a ball back and forth)	The key-person role allows children to experience a balance of adult-led activities and learning opportunities while having the freedom to explore their environment with the knowledge that they are safe and secure.
22–36 months	• Interested in others' play and starting to join in • Seeks out others to share experiences • Shows affection and concern for people who are special to them • May form a special friendship with another child	Children become more sociable as they grow and are able to show genuine concern for each other when, for example, someone is upset or hurt. They start to realise that their actions and the actions of others have consequences. Explore emotions through stories, songs and mirror play. Small group activities and role-play experiences allow children to form special friendships.

Age Group	EYFS Learning Outcomes	Activities and Ideas for Best Practice
30–50 months	• Can play in a group, extending and elaborating play ideas (e.g. building up a role-play activity with other children) • Initiates play, offering cues to peers to join them • Keeps play going by responding to what others are saying or doing • Demonstrates friendly behaviour, initiating conversations and forming good relationships with peers and familiar adults	Enhancing continuous provision areas following children's interests enables children to see similarities in likes and dislikes and further develops friendships. Children are able to retell experiences and extend language scaffolding each other's play.
40–60 months	• Initiates conversations, attends to and takes account of what others say • Explains own knowledge and understanding, and asks appropriate questions of others • Takes steps to resolve conflicts with other children (e.g. finding a compromise) **Early Learning Goal** Children play cooperatively, taking turns with others. They take account of one another's ideas about how to organise their activity. They show sensitivity to others' needs and feelings, and form positive relationships with adults and other children.	Gathering/circle time provides opportunities for children to gain important listening and turn-taking experience enabling them to value each other's input, opinions and thoughts. Consistency in behavioural expectations allows children to see an environment that supports all children and creates a culture of fairness. Allowing time and encouraging children to find solutions to problems and resolve their own conflicts encourages children to find compromises that are fair.

SELF-CONFIDENCE AND AWARENESS

This table explores personal, social and emotional development in the context of self-confidence and awareness.

Age Group	EYFS Learning Outcomes	Activities and Ideas for Best Practice
Birth to 26 months	• Laughs and gurgles (e.g. shows pleasure at being tickled and other physical interactions) • Uses voice, gesture, eye contact and facial expression to make contact with people and keep their attention • Enjoys finding own nose, eyes or tummy as part of naming games • Learns that own voice and actions have effects on others • Uses pointing with eye gaze to make requests, and to share an interest • Engages other person to help achieve a goal (e.g. to get an object out of reach) • Explores new toys and environments, but 'checks in' regularly with familiar adult as and when needed • Gradually able to engage in pretend play with toys (supports child to understand that their own thinking may be different from others) • Demonstrates sense of self as an individual (e.g. wants to do things independently, says 'no' to adult)	Building self-confidence and self-esteem through the key-person system enables children to express their feelings, needs and wants through effective communication such as: • pointing • copying • gesturing • start of speech/babble. Role-play, home corner and pretend play with puppets encourages imagination.

Age Group	EYFS Learning Outcomes	Activities and Ideas for Best Practice

22–36 months	• Separates from main carer with support and encouragement from a familiar adult
	• Expresses own preferences and interests
		The key-person system supports separation from main carers and families by ensuring that there is always a familiar person who understands the child's needs and wants.
		
		Children's voices and opinions should be heard and seen around the setting through:
		   • displays
		   • artwork
		   • pictures from home
		   • environment enhancements.

30–50 months	• Can select and use activities and resources with help • Welcomes and values praise for what they have done • Enjoys responsibility of carrying out small tasks • Is more outgoing towards unfamiliar people and more confident in new social situations • Confident to talk to other children when playing, and will communicate freely about own home and community • Shows confidence in asking adults for help	Continuous provision allows children to self-select resources that they are interested in and use them in a way that suits the purpose of their play. Resources should be varied, promote challenge and be at child height.

| 40–60 months | • Confident to speak to others about own needs, wants, interests and opinions
• Can describe self in positive terms and talk about abilities

Early Learning Goal
Children are confident to try new activities and say why they like some activities more than others. They are confident to speak in a familiar group, will talk about their ideas and will choose the resources they need for their chosen activities. They say when they do or don't need help. | Gathering/circle time is a perfect time to introduce a show-and-tell structure to encourage children to speak freely about their interests, likes, dislikes and experiences.

Linking these interests to areas of continuous provision and planning will also support children's confidence. |

MANAGING FEELINGS AND BEHAVIOUR

This table explores personal, social and emotional development in the context of managing feelings and behaviour.

Age Group	EYFS Learning Outcomes	Activities and Ideas for Best Practice
Birth to 26 months	<ul><li>Is comforted by touch and people's faces and voices</li><li>Seeks physical and emotional comfort by snuggling in to trusted adults</li><li>Calms from being upset when held, rocked, spoken or sung to with soothing voice</li><li>Shows a range of emotions such as pleasure, fear and excitement</li><li>Reacts emotionally to other people's emotions (e.g. smiles when smiled at and becomes distressed if hears another child crying)</li><li>Uses familiar adult to share feelings, such as excitement or pleasure, and for 'emotional refuelling' when feeling tired, stressed or frustrated</li><li>Growing ability to soothe themselves, and may like to use a comfort object</li><li>Cooperates with care-giving experiences (e.g. dressing)</li><li>Beginning to understand 'yes', 'no' and some boundaries</li></ul>	The key-person system fosters feelings of security and warmth between child and key person. The key person encourages positive behaviour and has consistent boundaries for each child enabling children to follow routines and be respectful towards each other and their environment. Books, stories, puppet play and songs about emotions help children to understand how they feel and how to manage their emotions in a positive way.

- Is aware of others' feelings (e.g. looks concerned if hears crying or looks excited if hears a familiar happy voice)
- Growing sense of will and determination may result in feelings of anger and frustration, which are difficult to handle (e.g. may have tantrums)
- Responds to a few appropriate boundaries, with encouragement and support
- Begins to learn that some things are theirs, some things are shared and some things belong to other people

★

Age Group	EYFS Learning Outcomes	Activities and Ideas for Best Practice
22–36 months	• Seeks comfort from familiar adults when needed • Can express their own feelings such as sadness, happiness, anger, fear, worry • Responds to the feelings and wishes of others • Aware that some actions can hurt or harm others • Tries to help or give comfort when others are distressed • Shows understanding and cooperates with some boundaries and routines • Can inhibit own actions/behaviours (e.g. stop themselves from doing something they shouldn't do) • Growing ability to distract self when upset (e.g. by engaging in a new play activity)	Building on the positive experiences that have been established, children are able to demonstrate growing control over their emotions and are able to distract themselves when feeling frustrated or upset. Sharing information and key policies, such as supporting positive behaviour with parents, will help to ensure that all adults within the child's life respond to behaviour in a similar way.
30–50 months	• Aware of own feelings, and knows that some actions and words can hurt others' feelings • Begins to accept the needs of others and can take turns and share resources, sometimes with support from others • Can usually tolerate delay when needs are not immediately met, and understands wishes may not always be met • Can usually adapt behaviour to different events, social situations and changes in routine	Providing children with a wide range of experiences allows them to understand how to behave in social situations. Create ways for children to show each other how they feel using a feelings tree: • persona dolls • emotion cards. Turn-taking games and group activities encourage listening, attention and patience.

| 40–60 months | • Understands that own actions affect other people (e.g. becomes upset or tries to comfort another child when they realise they have upset them)

• Aware of the boundaries set, and of behavioural expectations in the setting

• Beginning to be able to negotiate and solve problems without aggression (e.g. when someone has taken their toy)

Early Learning Goal

Children talk about how they and others show feelings, talk about their own and others' behaviour and its consequences, and know that some behaviour is unacceptable. They work as part of a group or class, and understand and follow the rules. They adjust their behaviour to different situations and take changes of routine in their stride. | Encourage children to make their own rules based on how they would like to be treated within the setting. These rules can then be displayed at child height and become a talking point for children, staff and groups.

Allowing time and encouraging children to find solutions to problems and resolve their own conflicts encourages children to find compromises that are fair. |

CHAPTER 4

PREVENT DUTY

The Counter Terrorism and Security Act was introduced in July 2015. Part of the Act known as the 'Prevent Duty' places a duty on registered providers and authorities to prevent people from being drawn into terrorism. The guidance states:

> Early Years' providers serve arguably the most vulnerable and impressionable members of society. The Early Years' Foundation Stage (EYFS) accordingly places clear duties on providers to keep children safe and promote their welfare. It makes clear that to protect children in their care, providers must be alert to any safeguarding and child protection issues in the child's life at home or elsewhere. (3.4 EYFS) Early Years' providers must take action to protect children from harm and should be alert to harmful behaviour by other adults in the child's life.

This statement acknowledges how important Early Years' providers are in having a positive influence and safeguarding children and young people. The duty does not suggest that children within Early Years' settings are extremists, but it does demonstrate that children, even the very young, can become victims of radicalisation and extremist ideology through the influence of others. There are many ways this may be done such as the purposeful segregation from other people of different cultures or beliefs, through teachings that do not support British values or by being taken to other countries where extremist ideologies are promoted.

The statement also shows that the youngest children are the most vulnerable, further demonstrating that the work in preventing children from becoming radicalised starts with early years. As settings, we need to ensure that we use 'professional personalisation' of services and relationships with children's immediate and wider families to promote the welfare of the children.

PROFESSIONAL PERSONALISATION

All settings strive to be as professional as they can be. We have legal duties to fulfil, policies and procedures to follow and a code of conduct that ensures all staff remain professional. However, there is a very human part of our work which dictates that we want to do the very best we can for the children and families we serve.

As settings, we are encouraged to make strong links with parents and families through the EYFS, and our Ofsted grading depends upon the creation of these effective partnerships. Practitioners are potentially able to see parents/carers twice a day for conversations, exchange written information through daily diaries and more often than not have an in-depth knowledge of family circumstances. The closeness of these relationships are rarely mimicked in the school system; parents drop off at the school gates at 9.00 a.m. and collect at 3.30 p.m., meeting only with teachers at parents' evenings or if a problem arises. The ability to offer professional personalisation is one of the reasons why Early Years is uniquely placed to act upon the Prevent Duty.

It is helpful for practitioners to understand the scope of the Counter Terrorism and Security Act, particularly as it pertains to extremism and radicalisation. By having a broad understanding of the risks and potential vulnerability, you are better equipped to notice any warning signs and how to report them.

It is good practice for all members of staff to have undertaken training to further their understanding of the Prevent Duty and increase their knowledge of signs and reporting procedures.[1]

EXTREMISM AND RADICALISATION

The Prevent Duty guidance consistently uses the terms extremism and radicalisation, but what do they mean?

'Radicalisation' refers to the process by which a person comes to support terrorism and forms of extremism leading to terrorism. During that process it is possible to intervene to prevent vulnerable people being drawn into terrorist-related activity.

'Extremism' is vocal or active opposition to fundamental British Values, including democracy, the rule of law, individual liberty and mutual respect and tolerance of different faiths and beliefs. We also include in our definition of extremism calls for the death of members of our armed forces, whether in this country or overseas. Terrorist groups very often draw on extremist ideas developed by extremist organisations. (Prevent Duty, DFE, July 2015)

---

1   Free online channel training is available at http://course.ncalt.com/ Channel_General_Awareness/01/index.html.

HOW DO PEOPLE BECOME DRAWN INTO TERRORISM?

People are more susceptible to being drawn into extremist ideology when they feel they can identify with, or have a connection to, a certain cause or to the people serving the cause. Anyone from any background, faith or culture could be drawn into extremist ideology as there is no single profile that dictates who will become radicalised. However, there are known factors that increase the possibility of someone being drawn into terrorism. These factors include:

- peer pressure

- Internet

- crime and anti-social behaviour

- family tensions

- race or hate crime

- lack of self-esteem or identity

- personal or political grievances.

A single factor alone does not mean that someone will be drawn into terrorism, but the more factors involved, the greater the possibility.

RESPONSIBILITIES UNDER THE PREVENT DUTY

Early Years has a duty to have 'due regard to the need to prevent people from being drawn into terrorism'. We do this through (a) identification, (b) reporting concerns, (c) building self-confidence and self-esteem and (d) risk assessment, so that children are able to challenge extremist ideology.

Identification

It is the duty of each practitioner to ensure they are able to identify children and families who are vulnerable to radicalisation. As there is no single profile of what to look for in cases of suspected radicalisation, we look (as we would with any safeguarding concern) for changes in behaviour, attitudes and routines, not only in the children but also siblings and extended family.

Changes that are out of character could include:

- change in dress, for example from hijab to niqab or burka

- changing friendship groups

- changing habits such as not eating certain meats

- wearing signs of ideology

- changes in demeanour and/or mannerisms

- comments that are against the principles of British values

- open support for terrorist activity – either through the avocation of a physical attack or support for those who are going to fight.

Reporting concerns

All practitioners should know how to report a concern regarding the Prevent Duty. Contact details and procedure should be clearly detailed within the setting's safeguarding policy. The policy should state who in the Local Safeguarding Children's Board and Multi Agency Safeguarding Hub (LSCB/MASH) to contact as well as their telephone and email details. It is also necessary to include contact details for your local channel police officer and the national contact details for the government's **Channel** initiative. Channel is the early intervention strategy that is part of the government's **Contest** counter-terrorism strategy.

Contest has four aims:

1. Prevent: Prevent people from being drawn into extremist ideology.

2. Pursue: Disrupt and/or stop terror threats – seeking prosecution where possible.

3. Protect: Strengthen our protection against a terror threat both in the UK and our overseas protectorates.

4. Prepare: Reduce the possible impact where an attack cannot be stopped.

Channel is a key part of Contest as it provides an assessment of vulnerability for those being drawn in to terrorism. Radicalisation does not happen quickly; it takes time to embed thoughts and ideas. It is during this time where the Channel programme aims to intervene. Once a referral has been made, the Channel police practitioner will conduct an initial assessment. This preliminary assessment will look specifically at the individual's engagement of potential terrorist activity, their intent to harm and their capability to carry out a terror-related event. Information will be gathered from other professionals, such as local authorities, police and the voluntary sector, to create an informed picture.

Engagement looks at how actively engaged someone is in an ideology. Are they members of groups, organisations or online communities? Channel will look at the views of the groups and their political and cultural standpoints. These factors on their own are not always negative. Most people do not want to harm others because of an ideology.

Intent takes engagement one step further and can be displayed through verbal threats and/or warnings directed at non-members of the ideology such as different faiths, Westerners and/or political institutions.

Capability means that in order to carry out an act of terror, skills, resources and networks are required. For example, if a nurse wanted to plant a bomb, they may not have the necessary skills to do so, but someone who is a chemist or has a background in the military would. If the individual does not have the skills, they may seek out those who do.

Once the assessment has taken place, Channel will decide if the early intervention programme is appropriate for them. If it isn't appropriate, the individual may be signposted to other services.

As with any safeguarding concern, it is the role of the practitioner to report your concerns and allow the authorities to make their decisions based on all of the evidence.

Building self-confidence and self-esteem

As practitioners, we understand the importance of building children's self-confidence and how having a strong sense of self can have a positive impact throughout life. The EYFS gives us a framework to promote self-confidence and positive relationships through the aspect of personal, social and emotional development.

TRAINING: COACHING AND MENTORING

Settings should provide training to ensure that all practitioners are able to feel confident in their understanding of the Prevent Duty. This can be done through face-to-face delivery, private online training or government modules such as the 'Channel Awareness' training module. All of these approaches need to be followed through with coaching and mentoring to make sure that the information has been embedded within your practice.

Risk assessment

All settings must conduct a risk assessment to demonstrate that they fully understand the risks affecting children and young people in their own geographical area, the potential likelihood of them being drawn into extremism, how they support these vulnerable groups and the reporting procedures of the setting. Most information can be found from the national office of statistics or from local authority websites.

An example of a risk assessment is given below for you to adapt to your own setting, and you can access a template to print at www.jkp.com/voucher using the code MADDOCKVALUES.

PREVENT DUTY RISK ASSESSMENT/ACTION PLAN

No.	Prevent Vulnerability/Risk Area	Risk (Y/N)	Action Taken or Already in Place to Mitigate/Address Risk	Responsible Person	When	Red, Amber, Green
1	**Leadership** Do the following people have a good understanding of their own and institutional responsibilities in relation to the Prevent Duty: • board of governors • nursery management • practitioners • support staff • safeguarding team?					
2	**Partnership** Is there active engagement from the institution's governors, safeguarding team, managers and leaders? Does the setting have an identified single point of contact in relation to Prevent Duty? Does the setting engage with the local authority, police Prevent Leads and with local Prevent boards/steering groups? Is this information clearly stated in your policy?					

No.	Prevent Vulnerability/Risk Area	Risk (Y/N)	Action Taken or Already in Place to Mitigate/Address Risk	Responsible Person	When	Red, Amber, Green
3	**Staff Training** Do all staff have sufficient knowledge and confidence to: • exemplify British values in their daily practice, parental involvement and commitment to teaching • understand the factors that make people vulnerable to being drawn into terrorism and to challenge extremist ideas which are used by terrorist groups and can purport to legitimise terrorism • have sufficient training to be able to recognise this vulnerability and be aware of what action to take in response?					
4	**Safety Online** Does the setting have a policy relating to the use of IT and does it contain a specific reference and inclusion of the Prevent Duty? Does the setting employ filtering/firewall systems to prevent staff, students and visitors from accessing extremist websites and material? Does this also include the use of their own devices via Wi-Fi?					

5	**Safeguarding**	
	Is protection against the risk of radicalisation and extremism included within Safeguarding and other relevant policies?	
	Do all staff, including designated leads, receive additional and ongoing training to enable the effective understanding and handling of referrals relating to radicalisation and extremism?	
	Does the institution utilise Channel as a support mechanism in cases of radicalisation and extremism?	
6	**Communications**	
	Is the setting's Prevent Lead and their role widely known across the institution?	
	Are staff and students made aware of the Prevent Duty, current risks and appropriate activities in this area?	
	Are there information-sharing protocols in place to facilitate information sharing with Prevent partners?	

No.	Prevent Vulnerability/Risk Area	Risk (Y/N)	Action Taken or Already in Place to Mitigate/Address Risk	Responsible Person	When	Red, Amber, Green
7	**Incident Management** Does the institution have a critical incident management plan which is capable of dealing with terrorist-related issues? Is a suitably trained and informed person identified to lead on the response to such an incident?					
8	**Staff and Volunteers** Does awareness training extend to sub-contracted staff and volunteers? Is the institution vigilant to the radicalisation of staff by sub-contracted staff and volunteers?					

Action Plan created by_____   Signed_____   Date_____

Plan disseminated to team: Yes / No   Date_____

—— CHAPTER 5 ——

UNDERSTANDING OF THE WORLD

Understanding of the world is divided into the two subcategories of (a) people and communities and (b) technology. In this chapter we explore how we can demonstrate the ethos of British values through the teaching and supporting of children's understanding of the world. As we know children learn best through experience, it is important that we create opportunities and experiences that not only reflect their own experiences and culture but also the experiences and cultures of the local community and the wider global community in which we all live.

You can access templates of the tables that follow to print at www.jkp.com/voucher using the code MADDOCKVALUES.

PEOPLE AND COMMUNITIES

This table explores understanding of the world in the context of people and communities.

Age Group	EYFS Learning Outcomes	Activities and Ideas for Best Practice
Birth to 26 months	• Begins understanding of people and communities through early attachment and other relationships • Is curious about people and shows interest in stories about themselves and their family • Enjoys pictures and stories about themselves, their families and other people	Children should be able to see themselves and familiar people around their environment. This will help them to have a sense of belonging and feel valued in the setting. Some of the ways this can be achieved include setting-created albums and storybooks of children's: • home • family • familiar people • pets • outings • holidays • other children • members of staff. Supplement fictitious names in songs and rhymes for the names of the children and staff. Put pictures on storage areas, such as lockers and pegs, so the children can identify themselves and their belongings independently.
22–36 months	• Has a sense of own immediate family and relations	It is important for children and families to have a sense of belonging. Displaying photos of the children and their families at play and at home will encourage this sense of belonging.

- In pretend play, imitates everyday actions and events from own family and cultural background (e.g. making and drinking tea) - Beginning to have their own friends - Learns that they have similarities and differences that connect them to, and distinguish them from, others	Including a wide variety of resources in continuous provision areas allows the unfamiliar to become familiar and extends learning opportunities; for example, in the home corner, resources could include: • chopsticks, woks, wooden bowls, mortar and pestle, packets, tins and jars from around the world, menus and labelling in different languages • menus and cooking activities that include world foods on a regular basis, which gives inspiration for children to recreate what they have eaten and/or made • clothing and materials that reflect the local and international community.
	Support and encourage children to make friends in small groups using adult-led activities.
	Encourage buddy system for settling children.
	Engage in team-building games such as mini Olympics.
	Support each other and celebrate successes and achievements.
	Encourage them to create portraits of themselves, their families and other children in the setting and in the global community.
	Promote displays and resources that reflect the children in the setting and the wider community.
	Make mirrors freely available so children can independently explore similarities and differences.
	Encourage creation of jigsaws of themselves and others.
	Promote books, displays and resources that reflect the heritage of the children and families in the local setting and the wider global community.

★

Age Group	EYFS Learning Outcomes	Activities and Ideas for Best Practice
30–50 months	• Shows interest in the lives of people who are familiar to them	Children are primarily interested in themselves first, then those who are closest to them. Utilise these differences in your children and families to promote interest and exploration.
	• Remembers and talks about significant events in their own experience	Ask parents to come into nursery to share skills such as telling stories in different languages, interesting occupations, gardening, cooking and so forth.
		Singing songs and rhymes in different languages.
	• Recognises and describes special times or events for family or friends	Allow children time to tell each other what they have done/liked or disliked on a daily basis.
		Create a timeline of special events past, present and future.
	• Shows interest in different occupations and ways of life	Provide opportunities for children to recall and retell celebrations and events.
		Encourage visits to your setting from people of different occupations.
	• Knows some of the things that make them unique, and can talk about some of the similarities and differences in relation to friends or family	Encourage visits to different places of work.
		Provide role-play opportunities for different occupations.
		Provide a wide range of books, DVDs, CDs, ICT games and resources that promote age, gender and cultural diversity in occupations.
		Create tally charts with the group demonstrating similarities and differences in areas such as hair colour, eye colour, areas in which they live, pets, likes, dislikes and so forth.

40–60 months	• Enjoys joining in with family customs and routines	Meaningfully explore traditions and customs of other cultures using foods, music, dance, stories, outings and so forth.
	Early Learning Goal Children talk about past and present events in their own lives and in the lives of family members. They know that other children don't always enjoy the same things, and are sensitive to this. They know about similarities and differences between themselves and others, and among families, communities and traditions.	Children learn empathy, understanding and how to value the opinions of others through experience. Creating a culture of positive role modelling, clear expectations and valuing the participation of each child will further support learning.

THE WORLD

This table explores understanding of the world in the context of the surrounding environment.

Age Group	EYFS Learning Outcomes	Activities and Ideas for Best Practice
Birth to 26 months	• Moves eyes, then head, to follow moving objects • Reacts with abrupt change when a face or object suddenly disappears from view • Looks around a room with interest; visually scans environment for novel, interesting objects and events • Smiles with pleasure at recognisable playthings • Repeats actions that have an effect (e.g. kicking or hitting a mobile or shaking a rattle) • Closely observes what animals, people and vehicles do • Watches toy being hidden and tries to find it • Looks for dropped objects	Children learn about the world through experience and they experience the world around them through their senses. It is particularly important to provide opportunities for babies and young children to explore using all of their senses. Support sensory exploration through: • heuristic and treasure baskets • scented herb bags • gloop, flour, pasta • music and musical instruments.

• Becomes absorbed in combining objects (e.g. banging two objects or placing objects into containers) • Knows things are used in different ways (e.g. a ball for rolling or throwing, a toy car for pushing) Explores objects by linking together different approaches: shaking, hitting, looking, feeling, tasting, mouthing, pulling, turning and poking • Remembers where objects belong • Matches parts of objects that fit together (e.g. puts lid on teapot)	Create realistic small-world environments using natural materials (e.g. having hay, grass and soil for the farm). Create opportunities for children to plan and change their own environments both inside and outside based on their own ideas and interests.
22–36 months • Enjoys playing with small-world models such as a farm, a garage, or a train track • Notices detailed features of objects in their environment	Create opportunities to explore recurring patterns such as changes in traffic lights.

Age Group	EYFS Learning Outcomes	Activities and Ideas for Best Practice
30–50 months	• Comments and asks questions about aspects of their familiar world such as the place where they live or the natural world • Can talk about some of the things they have observed such as plants, animals, natural and found objects • Talks about why things happen and how things work • Develops an understanding of growth, decay and changes over time • Shows care and concern for living things and the environment	Create a map of the local area with places of interest including the setting, schools, shops, parks, beaches and community hubs. Demonstrate the size and position of the local area within the country and global maps. Explore places around the world where children have visited or where extended family may live. Ask parents if they have any memorabilia they could share with the setting. Eye-spy walks, welly walks, listening walks, math and phonic walks. Engage in forest school activities. Create areas for natural art displays both indoors and outdoors. Create an area for taking mechanical objects apart and putting them back together using real tools and equipment.

Engage in weather-cycle exploration and experiments, for example:

- why the sun shines in different parts of the sky at different times of the day
- tracing shadows on the floor
- the affect of heat on ice
- use and making of windmills to explore the direction and speed of wind
- collection of rain in measured pots.

Engage in life-cycle projects such as chick and butterfly hatching and tadpole evolution.

Promote activities to support understanding of how humans grow from babies into children, adolescents, adults, elderly.

Engage in making one's own compost.

Participate in plant, fruit and vegetable growing.

Consider having a nursery pet.

Promote recycling activities.

Age Group	EYFS Learning Outcomes	Activities and Ideas for Best Practice
40–60 months	• Looks closely at similarities, differences, patterns and change **Early Learning Goal** Children know about similarities and differences in relation to places, objects, materials and living things. They talk about the features of their own immediate environment and how environments might vary from one another. They make observations about animals and plants and explain why some things occur, and talk about changes.	Encourage children to look for similarities and differences in each other and other cultures. Providing opportunities to compare where the children live and the rest of the world could include: • weather cycles • seasons • animals • houses • languages • money • schools/Early Years' settings.

TECHNOLOGY

This table explores understanding of the world in the context of technology.

Age Group	EYFS Learning Outcomes	Activities and Ideas for Best Practice
Birth to 26 months	• Begins understanding technology through exploring and making sense of objects and how they behave • Anticipates repeated sounds, sights and actions (e.g. when an adult demonstrates an action toy several times) • Shows interest in toys with buttons, flaps and simple mechanisms, and begins to learn to operate them	Baby rooms/areas should be equipped with a range of equipment that promotes curiosity and exploration such as: • lift-the-flap books • books with sound effects • touch-and-feel books • ICT toys with lights and sounds • telephones.
22–36 months	• Seeks to acquire basic skills in turning on and operating some ICT equipment • Operates mechanical toys (e.g. turns the knob on a wind-up toy or pulls back on a friction car)	Outdoor areas present a fantastic opportunity to create areas for children to operate equipment such as wheels, pulley systems and large scales for weighing and comparing. A wide range of friction toys should be available.

Age Group	EYFS Learning Outcomes	Activities and Ideas for Best Practice
30–50 months	• Knows how to operate simple equipment (e.g. turns on CD player and uses remote control) • Shows an interest in technological toys with knobs or pulleys, or real objects such as cameras or mobile phones • Shows skill in making toys work by pressing parts or lifting flaps to achieve effects such as sound, movements or new images • Knows that information can be retrieved from computers	Allow children to take photographs of their environment both in the setting and when on walks, then display these photographs at child height around the setting. Encourage children when out and about to press buttons such as pelican crossings, doorbells and intercom systems.
40–60 months	• Completes a simple program on a computer • Uses ICT hardware to interact with age-appropriate computer software **Early Learning Goal** Children recognise that a range of technology is used in places such as homes and schools. They select and use technology for particular purposes.	There are an increasing number of settings that use computer tablets or other touch-screen technology. This type of technology has its place, though it is important to remember that hand/eye coordination can be supported effectively by using a mouse on a personal computer, and hand strength and dexterity can be supported by pressing the keys on a keyboard. Have a range of games to support development across all areas of learning that are age appropriate and provide challenge. Allowing children to access the computer on their own and freely choose their own software will encourage independence, freedom of choice and decision-making processes.

CHAPTER 6

CASE STUDIES

The Early Years' Foundation Stage tells us what we need to do to fulfil our statutory duty, but it does not tell us how to do it. This leaves the framework open for our own individual interpretation. Inevitably this will lead to a variety in the quality of practice.

In this chapter we hear the views and experiences of Early Years' settings and childminders who are currently working within the common inspection framework.

BRITISH VALUES CASE STUDY 1: KING DAVID KINDERGARTEN, LIVERPOOL

Could you describe your provision?

We are a purpose-built private kindergarten which is managed by a governing body, the King David and Harold House Foundation. Democracy, Rule of Law, Individual Liberty, and Mutual Respect and Tolerance have always been part of the ethos of the kindergarten.

There are three classrooms which are bright and attractively designed. The children are able to choose from a wide selection of attractive learning activities, which are accessible to the children from low-level, child-friendly units, allowing them to gain independence in readiness for school. The rooms are designed to enhance free play to the outdoor area where lots of planting and harvesting happen. The outdoor area allows the children to freely use their imagination and gain lots of transferable skills. All three rooms have interactive whiteboards.

The kindergarten is registered for 80 children serving both the Jewish community and the surrounding areas. The kindergarten prides itself on being an inclusive and welcoming kindergarten where children attend from other cultures. Parents/ carers are invited to talk to the children about how their culture is celebrated. All the children learn about the Jewish festivals and love creating the special artwork and delicacies to take home.

There is a wide range of percussion instruments which the children love to use to accompany them when singing or doing drama sessions. A sensory room, which some of the children call 'The Magic Room', allows the children to experience lots of different sensory areas.

There is a drop-off and buggy-park facility for parents/ carers.

How did you feel when you learned that settings were being asked to promote British values and would be inspected on them?

Reading what kindergartens were being asked to promote in the British values document, I felt we were already meeting the requirements.

Did it make any difference to your provision? If so what changes did you make?

The only difference that it has made is that we have produced a document, which is available to parents, explaining how the kindergarten teaches British values.

Did you or your team require any additional support or training?

Our team went through the document together and were confident that the values listed were being underpinned in the kindergarten.

How well do you feel the terms Democracy, Rule of Law, Individual Liberty, and Mutual Respect and Tolerance describe British values?

I think they describe what is expected from both adults and children at a basic level.

Do you think that by promoting British values this will have an impact upon children and society in general?

I would like to think it will happen. Unfortunately, we are living in a society which seems to have lost sight of the fundamental difference between right and wrong.

How have you included and informed your parents and families of British values, and what are their views?

We displayed the booklet we produced on how we support British values at the kindergarten. In addition to this, I will email a copy to all parents. New parents will receive a copy in their pack.

If you could redefine the term 'British values' or the headings that underpin British values, what would they be?

I think the title and headings are OK.

Do you think the changes that have been made to Early Years are reflected in the practice of education as a whole and wider government departments?

I think some of the ideas which have been introduced are very good.

Do you think the term 'British values' is inclusive of the diverse cultures we find in Britain today?

I think this would depend on advice given from representatives of diverse cultures and how acceptable the document would be to people from different cultures.

Do you feel you are able to keep your identity as a faith school while still actively promoting British values?

We have always promoted the values detailed in the document and it has never affected the identity of the kindergarten.

BRITISH VALUES CASE STUDY 2: STARS CHILDCARE, MERSEYSIDE

Could you describe your provision?

Stars Childcare offers care for children between the ages of 0 and 11 years. We have a room for toddlers and preschool as well as a facility for afterschool club and holiday club. We have just recently opened a baby room.

How did you feel when you learned that settings were being asked to promote British values and would be inspected on them?

British values are something that we instill in our children through the everyday care and learning that we provide. However, it has given us a focus on some of the activities/themes that we plan for throughout the year.

Did it make any difference to your provision? If so, what changes did you make?

We updated our policies and procedures and a 'British values' board has been set up in the room. We have a 'British values' project that our Holiday Club children can participate in during the holidays.

Did you or your team require any additional support or training?

We updated our knowledge online and through information passed on to us from the Early Years' team. We have also had one-to-one discussions with our manager.

How well do you feel the terms Democracy, Rule of Law, Individual Liberty, and Mutual Respect and Tolerance describe British values?

I feel these themes describe British values well, although they are not clear to all children.

Do you think that by promoting British values, this will have an impact upon children and society in general?

Settings should already be promoting British values through the everyday planning, activities and resources they provide for children. However, now there is more of a focus, so it should have more of an impact.

How have you included and informed your parents and families of British values and what are their views?

Parents/carers have been informed through the newsletters, and their ideas and contribution are always welcome. They particularly like the fact that their children experience other cultures and celebrate other festivals from around the world.

If you could redefine the term 'British values' or the headings that underpin British values, what would they be?

For children in Early Years, I do feel the terms need to be simplified. For example, I might choose these headings [or something similar]: 'Making Choices', 'Respecting Others', 'Rules', 'Our Views' and 'Self-Confidence'.

Do you think the changes that have been made to Early Years are reflected in the practice of education as a whole and wider government departments?

I'm not entirely sure if the changes are completely reflected by the wider government departments as I do not fully believe that there is always mutual respect or freedom of speech within our society. However, I do believe that the values are reflected [as much as they can be] in education within schools and Early

Years. The problems occur when children become influenced by other factors [especially in the media], and this is something that the government needs to address in this country.

Do you think the term 'British values' is inclusive of the diverse cultures we find in Britain today?

'British values' illustrates the basic human qualities that everyone should aspire to have regardless of religion, culture, race and so forth; therefore, it should reflect all people of Britain.

Do you feel you are able to keep your identity as a non-faith/faith school while still actively promoting British values?

Yes, I do, and I think it's very important to keep the identity of the setting or school, as this is one of the main principles within British values: to 'respect other cultures and beliefs'.

BRITISH VALUES CASE STUDY 3: CHILDMINDERS

Could you describe your provision?

It is a selection of home-based settings caring for children 0–11 years.

How did you feel when you learned that settings were being asked to promote British values and would be inspected on them?

The majority of childminders felt that they had good practice but were unsure of what would happen in inspection and how they could prove they were actively promoting 'British values'.

Did it make any difference to your provision?
If so, what changes did you make?

Most childminders did not change anything within their provision.

Did you or your team require any
additional support or training?

Approximately half sought additional local authority and/or online training.

How well do you feel the terms Democracy,
Rule of Law, Individual Liberty, and Mutual
Respect and Tolerance describe British values?

The majority of childminders felt that the headings of Democracy, Rule of Law, Individual Liberty, and Mutual Respect and Tolerance cover British values, but the term 'British values' undermines the ethos of the headings.

Do you think that by promoting British values this will
have an impact upon children and society in general?

There was a feeling of optimism and hope that by promoting these values to both children and parents it would bring about greater respect for people as a whole.

How have you included and informed your parents
and families of British values, and what are their views?

Newsletters and informal conversations were the most popular ways of keeping parents informed of British values and any changes that were made to childminding settings.

If you could redefine the term 'British values' or the headings that underpin British values, what would they be?

The majority of childminders where happy with the headings, and only one would redefine them. As one childminder stated:

> I think that 'British values' are extremely important, but they aren't *just 'British'* values; they belong to everyone who has a conscience, and therefore to the majority of people and cultures. I think it should be called 'Common values' or 'Respectfulness'.

Do you think the changes that have been made to early years are reflected in the practice of education as a whole and wider government departments?

It was felt that education as a sector and in particular had made changes and recognised the requirement to actively promote British values; however, the wider government sectors do not appear to have made any changes or attempted to demonstrate their commitment to British values.

Do you think the term 'British values' is inclusive of the diverse cultures we find in Britain today?

Only half of childminders felt that British values was inclusive of other cultures, while some felt that the title of 'British values' actually made it divisive rather than inclusive. As one passionate childminder states:

> 'British values' are meant to teach us about diversity and inclusion. By calling it 'British values' it undermines the whole concept as it excludes everyone who isn't British!

Scrap the word 'British' from the title and we might just be getting somewhere.

Do you feel you are able to keep your identity as a non-faith/faith setting while still actively promoting British values?

The childminders felt that they were able to promote British values through being morally supportive but would not actively teach about religion.

CHAPTER 7

EXTERNAL VIEWPOINTS

In this chapter we will look at what Ofsted expects from settings and how your practice will be evaluated on inspection. We will also hear from an academic university lecturer and a local authority advisor on how the introduction of fundamental British values and the Prevent Duty has impacted upon their roles.

OFSTED

The new common inspection framework enables inspectors to base their judgement of settings upon the following headings:

- Quality of teaching and learning

- Leadership and management

- Personal development, behaviour and welfare

- Overall effectiveness

- Outcomes for children.

Each one provides opportunities for Early Years' settings to demonstrate their understanding of safeguarding and the Prevent Duty and how they actively promote British values.

It is important to remember that Ofsted do not have a hidden agenda when it comes to what they expect from settings or inspections. They have produced documents which set out exactly for what Ofsted inspectors will look and on what evidence they base their judgements:

- The EYFS Statutory Guidance and Development Matters[1] give us the things that as settings we must do by law in order to operate our settings. The development matters give us the areas of learning that we must promote including Personal, Social and Emotional Development and Understanding of the World.

- Early Years Inspection Handbook 2015[2] provides an evaluation schedule with clear grade descriptors for each outcome of 'outstanding', 'good', 'requires improvement' and 'inadequate'. Settings can make informed judgements using the evaluation schedule about their practice and see where there are areas of strength and areas for development.

  The table on pages 78–79 is an extract taken from the evaluation schedule in relation to British values.

- Inspecting Safeguarding in Early Years, Education and Skills 2015[3] gives specific expectations in relation to safeguarding, British values and the Prevent Duty. The inspector will be looking to see that policy and procedure and staff knowledge cover the following:

  » neglect

  » physical abuse

---

1   Available at https://www.gov.uk/government/publications/early-years-foundation-stage-framework--2.
2   Available at https://www.gov.uk/government/publications/early-years-inspection-handbook-from-september-2015.
3   Available at https://www.gov.uk/government/publications/inspecting-safeguarding-in-early-years-education-and-skills-from-september-2015.

» sexual abuse

» emotional abuse

» bullying, including online bullying and prejudice-based bullying

» racist, disability and homophobic or transphobic abuse

» gender-based violence and violence against women and girls

» radicalisation and/or extremist behaviour

» child sexual exploitation and trafficking

» the impact of new technologies on sexual behaviour, for example 'sexting'

» teenage relationship abuse

» substance misuse issues that may be specific to a local area or population, for example gang activity and youth violence

» domestic violence

» female genital mutilation

» forced marriage

» fabricated or induced illness

» poor parenting, particularly in relation to babies and young children

» other issues not listed here but that pose a risk to children, young people and vulnerable adults.

By making the most of our knowledge, experience and the tools that we have been given, we have the opportunity to demonstrate the very best practice when Ofsted arrive.

	Outstanding	Good	Requires Improvement	Inadequate
Leadership and Management	The promotion of equality, diversity and British values is at the heart of the setting's work. It is demonstrated through all its practices, including tackling any instances of discrimination and being alert to potential risks from radicalisation and extremism.	Leadership and managers actively promote equality, diversity and British values through all policies and practice. They tackle instances of discrimination effectively.	Leadership and management are not yet good. Any breaches of statutory requirements do not have a significant impact on children's safety, well-being or learning and development.	Leaders fail to recognise and/or tackle instances of discrimination. Equality, diversity and British values are not actively promoted in practice.
Quality of Teaching, Learning and Assessment	Practitioners provide an exceptional range of resources and activities that reflect and value the diversity of children's experiences. They actively challenge gender, cultural and racial stereotyping and help children gain an understanding of people, families and communities beyond their immediate experience.	Practitioners provide a wide range of opportunities for children to learn about people and communities beyond their immediate experience. Resources and activities reflect and value the diversity of children's backgrounds and experiences.	The provision is not yet good. Any breaches of the statutory requirements do not have a significant impact on children's learning and development.	Practitioners do not promote equality and diversity or extend children's understanding of communities beyond their immediate environment.

Personal Development, Behaviour and Welfare	Practitioners give children a wide range of experiences that promote understanding of people, families and communities beyond their own. They teach children the language of feelings and give them opportunities to reflect on their differences.	Children are learning to respect and celebrate each other's differences. They develop an understanding of diversity beyond their immediate family experience through a range of activities that teach them effectively about people in the wider world.	Provision to support children's personal development, behaviour and welfare is not yet good. Any breaches of the statutory requirements for safeguarding and welfare and/or learning and development do not have a significant impact on children's safety, well-being and personal development.	Children have a narrow experience that does not promote their understanding of people and communities beyond their own or help them to recognise and accept each other's differences.

EDUCATION

Linda Jones is an Early Years lecturer at Edge Hill University Liverpool. Linda sets out how the introduction of British values has impacted upon her teaching, and how she has adapted and will continue to adapt to British values going forward.

The original statement from Nicky Morgan referred to teaching children as young as two 'fundamental British values in an age-appropriate way to protect them from religious radicals'.

This entered the university classroom to be debated amongst Early Years' practitioners studying Foundation Degree and related BA Honours programmes. Fundamental British values (FBV) had seemingly appeared from nowhere, was vaguely defined and practitioners had no real sense, or initial guidance, of how to promote it. Fearful, that this 'new' area of practice would be sought out in forthcoming Ofsted inspections, they were keen to explore the term and understand how they could reflect this in practice. Initially, students worked in groups to unpick the terminology and then identify the many ways that children and adults make decisions together, how children were supported to develop their understanding of rules, and the associated Personal Social Emotional Development (PSED), Individual Liberty, was contextualised to Understanding the World, whilst Mutual Respect and Tolerance they defined as integral to diversity and related to gender, culture and racial stereotyping – before realising it was already being addressed within the EYFS.

In the coming months, the separate Prevent Duty and revision of the CIF meant that module content needed to feature the subject of FBV to identify what, where and how. Bespoke sessions now use group work and research to make links between high-quality practices in the EYFS, to recognise how children can be tangible, active partners in the Early Years' setting. Students develop their ability to engage in sustained shared thinking with children and learn how to promote strong parental partnerships to enable closer multi-faith, multi-lingual, multi-cultural partnerships to benefit their communities of practice.

However, more than the session content, the students themselves grew in confidence as they were able to explain FBV to their colleagues in their settings, cascading information, stimulating discourse amongst setting staff and managers. FBV is wrapped up in good practice and recognised within the EYFS. In the coming academic year, bespoke sessions will be built on responding to the positive feedback from these students, the pioneers of FBV in these university programmes.

LOCAL AUTHORITY

Neil Blumson is CPD Lead at Achieving for Children. He is also an active board member of NEYCTO, the National Early Years Consultants and Trainers organisation. Here he gives us an appraisal of what he has seen in practice since the introduction of British values, and the supportive role of the local authority going forward.

There's been quite a lot of work done in the Early Years' sector around what we mean when we talk about British values. It seems to have caused a lot of panic and misunderstanding.

If you Googled British values in Early Years a few months ago, there was a lot of misleading information posted by well-meaning practitioners. What don't we want to see and hear? British values doesn't mean that we all have to observe 'Fish and Chip Friday' or adorn our setting with Union flags! It doesn't mean that the children will be running the provision and making all of the decisions, and it doesn't mean that they will be telling adults what to do!

A little further down the road, it looks like practitioners are starting to get the message. We've tried to keep the message simple. Fundamental British values are embedded in the EYFS and have been since 2014. They are embedded in most of our practice already and have been for a long time. Practitioners just need to be able to share what they understand by British values with confidence.

In order to explain British values simply, we start with the Prevent Duty. It's the British values that underpin our work to keep children safe, promote their welfare and help them make good choices.

We already observe **Democracy**. A simple show of hands about which book children would like to hear or a discussion about how the home corner is going to be organised reinforces the value of children's views. The benefit in terms of supporting self-confidence is clear.

Rule of Law: There are rules everywhere, and children learn to follow them. They are applied consistently and fairly throughout the setting and throughout the day. Children learn that there are consequences to not following the rules in their setting. Importantly, they learn the difference between right and wrong and why we have these rules.

Individual Liberty: We watch and support our young children to develop their self-confidence and self-awareness. Most importantly we want them to have a positive sense of themselves. We support them in taking risks. We also want them to think about how their actions impact on those around them.

Mutual Respect and Tolerance of different faiths and beliefs are, and continue to be, underpinning principles of what we do.

When we break it down like this, it becomes clear that practitioners don't generally need to change what they do, they just need to be able to explain their practice within this context – just like they do within the context of the Prime and Specific Areas of Learning of the EYFS or Ages and Stages of Development. Ofsted will ask how it looks in practice, so let's be able to explain clearly and simply that we get it!

Looking forward, these underpinning principles will continue to be interwoven into our practitioner training, our network discussions and meetings so that we can continue to help our practitioners to feel confident and comfortable to understand, and be able to share with confidence, what *they* understand by 'British values'.

CLOSING THOUGHTS

British values is not a new concept. We as dedicated Early Years' professionals have for many years provided high-quality care and moral guidance to countless children. What is new is that we have the opportunity to showcase this practice on a practical level.

We are able through education to promote Fundamental British Values to our children, families and staff in the hope that in years to come we will see a society that is as inclusive as it is diverse. With every voice being heard and where 'Every Child Matters'.

PLANNING

Effective planning to encompass British values requires balance between international, national and local celebrations in order to make it meaningful to your setting and to the children. There seems to be little point in teaching Chinese New Year and Diwali if the local and community festivals are missed. Planning should be fun and challenging for all children, and it should include continuous provision, adult-led activities and outdoor experiences. Outlined here is an example planning sheet for September to August.

FESTIVALS THROUGHOUT THE YEAR

These festival are not exhaustive and dates change from year to year; however, having an annual plan means that festivals and celebrations can be planned for well in advance giving practitioners time to think of fun and interesting things to do.

September

World Teddy Bear Day

World Teddy Bear Day provides a perfect opportunity to celebrate these cuddly friends. Teddy bears took their names from Theodore Roosevelt who refused to kill a small bear while on a hunting trip.

Grandparents' Day

Grandparents' day is celebrated at different times in different countries. Cards, flowers and gifts are given as a way of thanking grandparents for everything that they do.

Rosh Hashanah

Rosh Hashanah is the first day of the Jewish new year of people and animals (there are four Jewish new years). It celebrates the creation of Adam and Eve. Traditionally there is the blowing of the Shofar (ram's horn) and eating of honeyed apples.

Mid Autumn (Moon) Festival

The Moon festival is an East Asian celebration of richness and togetherness. Traditionally families will have a special meal and eat moon cake.

Vijay Dashami (Dasera)

This Hindu festival makes the triumph of good over evil after a 10-day battle and concludes with the festival of Navarati. Celebrations include fireworks, the sharing of gifts and theatrical plays depicting the battle. This also celebrates the start of the harvest festival.

Ashura

This Islamic festival marks Noah's departure from the ark, the exodus of Moses from Egypt and the martyrdom of the Prophet Mohammed's grandson.

Yom Kippur

Yom Kippur is a day of atonement on the Jewish calendar. Many Jewish people spend the day visiting the synagogue in prayer or fasting. Once the fast is over, a special meal is shared.

October

Poetry Day

National poetry day is an initiative by the Forward Arts Foundation which aims to increase awareness of poetry and literacy.

Harvest

Harvest celebrates the gathering of crops before the winter. Typically schools and churches will collect food and then distribute it to the homeless and those members of the community less fortunate.

World Smile Day

World Smile Day came as the result of Harvey Ball's image of a smiley face becoming overused and, in his opinion, not being portrayed as the symbol of happiness and friendship that he imagined. The symbol was meant to inspire acts of kindness and friendship around the world.

Halloween

Halloween has its origins in pagan festivals held around the end of October in England, Wales, Scotland and Ireland. People believed that, at this time of year, the spirits of dead people could come 'alive' and walk among the living. They thought that it was important to dress up in costumes when venturing outside, to avoid being harmed by the spirits. This may be the origin of the Halloween costumes seen today. In Puritan times, Halloween celebrations were outlawed, but they were revived in later times.

All Souls' Day

Some churches, including the Catholic Church, hold special services with music and prayers focused on All Souls' Day on or around 2 November each year. It is a time for some Christians, including those who attend these special All Souls' Day services, to remember and pray for deceased family members and friends. Some people visit the graves of dead family or friends on All Souls' Day. All Souls' Day is closely associated with All Saints' Day (1 November), as both are known collectively as Hallowtide.

Diwali

Many activities and events are held in the United Kingdom to celebrate Diwali, which is known as the 'Festival of Lights'. Diwali is a time for spring cleaning in homes and offices. Many homes that celebrate Diwali have assorted sweets, savouries and Diwali herbs. Various lights, candles and sparklers are lit inside and outside homes.

November

Children in Need

Children in Need is a national fundraising campaign which raises money for sick and poor children in the United Kingdom and abroad. Organisations hold a variety of fundraising events including bake sales, sponsored events and pyjama days.

Nursery Rhyme Week

Nursery Rhyme Week aims to highlight the importance of rhythm and rhyme in children's language and literacy development.

Remembrance Sunday

Remembrance Sunday honours the heroic efforts, achievements and sacrifices that were made in past wars. People stop work to observe a moment of silence at 11 a.m. on 11 November, which is the time and date when hostilities formally ended after more than four years of battle during World War I. Poppies are worn as a symbol of respect and tribute on Remembrance Sunday and/or 11 November. The day is also marked by events such as memorial services, church services and parades. A national commemoration takes place at Whitehall, a road in the City of Westminster in central London.

St Andrew's Day

St Andrew is the patron saint of Scotland. He is said to have brought followers to Jesus from all over the world and encouraged the sharing of food among the people to whom he preached. St Andrew is also said to be the patron Saint of Cyprus, Poland and Romania. His life is celebrated with music, food and dance festivals which can last up to a week.

Bonfire Night

Bonfire Night celebrates the discovery of a plot by Guy Fawkes to blow up the houses of Parliament in London in 1605. Firework displays and bonfires are organised by local authorities.

December

Eid Milad ul-Nabi

Eid Milad ul-Nabi is an Islamic celebration of the life of the Prophet Mohammed. It falls on the twelfth or seventeenth day of the Islamic month of *Rabi' al-awwal*. The celebration is marked by fasting during the day with a special meal in the evening.

Chanukah

Chanukah celebrates the time where Syrian Greeks who had invaded Israel where defeated. When the Jewish people went to light the Menorah (Candelabra) in the temple, they found only one vial of olive oil. The oil which should have only lasted one day lasted eight days, which was enough time to prepare more oil. It was said to be a miracle, and so the festival of Chanukah was instituted. Traditional Chanukah customs include eating food prepared in oil, such as doughnuts and latkes (potato cakes), and playing games with a driedal (a type of spinning top).

Advent

The first Sunday in Advent is the Sunday closest to St Andrew's Day. This traditionally marks the start of the Christmas season. Christmas trees and decorations are put up, and Christmas cakes and puddings are made in preparation for Christmas Day.

Christmas

Christmas is a Christian holiday that celebrates the birth of Jesus. It is a time where families spend time together and there is a traditional exchange of presents. It is important that we continue to celebrate Christmas in a traditional way with Christmas trees, decorations and so forth while also explaining the meaning of Christmas in terms of sharing and caring for one another. We should consider how Christmas is celebrated around the world. For example, in Spain the traditional Christmas dinner is eaten on Christmas Eve and presents are given on 6 January, the day when the Three Wise Men were said to have given presents to the baby Jesus.

January

New Year

New Year is celebrated on 1 January each year. It is the start of the New Year in the Gregorian calendar. It is celebrated in many countries around the world by gatherings of families and friends who say goodbye to one year and welcome the start of a new year. Fireworks and festivities take place with a countdown to midnight.

Tu B'Shevat

Tu B'Shevat is a Jewish holiday that occurs on the fifteenth day of the Hebrew month of Shevat. It celebrates a 'new year of the trees'. Traditionally dried fruits and nuts, such as dates, figs, prunes and almonds, are eaten. In modern Israel it is seen as an ecological day, and trees, particularly eucalyptus trees, are planted.

Burns' Night

Burns' Night is celebrated in Scotland on or around 25 January. It commemorates the life of the bard (poet) Robert Burns who was born on 25 January 1759. The day also celebrates Burns' contribution to Scottish culture.

February

Shrove Tuesday

Many Christian churches in the United Kingdom observe Shrove Tuesday as the last day before the fast for the Lent period. It is traditionally the time when Christians ask for forgiveness and confess their sins. It is also known as Pancake Tuesday or Pancake Day.

Ash Wednesday

Ash Wednesday is a Christian day of penitence to cleanse the soul before fasting during the Lent period. Christians may attend special church services to receive the ash in the sign of the cross on their foreheads as a symbol of being sorry and repentant for their wrongdoings.

Chinese New Year

Chinese New Year celebrations can last for up to two weeks. Each year is symbolised by a different animal from the Chinese zodiac bringing the characteristics of that animal to anyone born in that year. Families get together and have special meals, and children receive red envelopes with money in them for luck.

Valentine's Day

Saint Valentine was imprisoned for conducting marriage ceremonies for soldiers who were forbidden to marry and for ministering to Christians. During his imprisonment he is said to have healed the sight of his jailer's daughter. On the eve of his execution, he wrote her a letter signed, 'Your Valentine'.

March
St David's Day

People in Wales and those of Welsh origin celebrate the life of their patron saint, St David, and the Welsh culture, on 1 March each year. Many people pin a daffodil or leek to their clothes, and some, especially children, wear traditional costumes.

World Book Day

World Book Day aims to spark children's interest in books by encouraging them to dress up as their favourite story character. The celebration was started by UNESCO. The date of 23 April was chosen as it is the anniversary of the death of William Shakespeare and other prominent authors.

Mothering Sunday

Mother's Day, or Mothering Sunday, is now a day to honour mothers and other mother figures, such as grandmothers, stepmothers and mothers-in-law. Many people make a special effort to visit their mother. They take cards and gifts to her and may treat her to brunch, lunch or high tea in a café, restaurant or hotel.

Holi Day

Holi is an Indian festival that celebrates the triumph of good over evil and the renewing of relationships. It is celebrated by the lighting of a bonfire on Holi Eve and the rubbing of 'Gulal' and 'Abeer' coloured paint into each other's faces.

Red Nose Day/Comic Relief

Red Nose Day is an annual fundraising campaign which uses comedy to raise money for vulnerable people both in the United Kingdom and abroad.

St Patrick's Day

St Patrick's Day celebrates the patron saint of Ireland. St Patrick is said to have banished all of the snakes from Ireland. It is traditionally celebrated by wearing a shamrock and getting together with friends.

Easter

Easter Sunday is a Christian celebration of the resurrection of Jesus. Many Christians go to mass or church services and exchange Easter eggs as a symbol of rebirth.

April

World Autism Day

World Autism Day aims to raise awareness of autism and the challenges that people with autism face. It is a day where fundraising takes place and blue is worn to show support.

St George's Day

St George's Day in England remembers St George, England's patron saint. The anniversary of his death, which is on 23 April, is seen as England's national day. According to legend, he was a soldier in the Roman army who killed a dragon and saved a princess.

Shakespeare Day

The day 23 April celebrates both the birth and death of William Shakespeare, one of England's greatest writers.

Rama Navami

Rama Navami celebrates the birth of Lord Rama, son of King Dasharatha of Ayodhya. The celebration begins with the thorough cleaning and the decoration of the house. Gifts of fruits and flowers are taken to the shrine of Rama and prayers are said.

Passover

Passover commemorates the liberation of the Jewish people from slavery in Egypt. It is celebrated with days of rest and special meals – called Seder – shared with family, friends and the poor, or those who live alone.

May

National Smile Month

National Smile Month is dedicated to improving oral health. Opportunities such as toothbrush swops, songs and rhymes, and visits from local dentists, are used by settings and schools to promote oral health awareness.

Buddha Day

Buddha Day celebrates the birth of Buddha. The celebration begins with the cleaning and decorating of homes. Statues of Buddha are washed as a reminder to wash away thoughts originating from greed and ignorance.

June

Father's Day

Father's Day is held on the third Sunday of June in the United Kingdom. It is a day to honour fathers and father figures, such as grandfathers and fathers-in-law. Many people make a special effort to visit their fathers or to send them a card or gifts.

Ramadan

Ramadan is an Islamic celebration. It celebrates when the first verses of the Koran were revealed to the Prophet Mohammed. Many Muslims will fast during daylight hours, having a meal before sunrise (Suhoor) and after sunset (Iftar).

July

National Childhood Obesity Week

National Childhood Obesity Week aims to increase awareness of the health-related problems that can happen as a result of being overweight and obese. Information and activities that promote physical activity and healthy nutrition are promoted through primary care trusts and children's centres.

American Independence Day

American Independence Day is an American celebration taking place on 4 July each year. It commemorates the day when the Declaration of Independence from the British Empire was signed in 1776. Fireworks, fairs, carnivals and concerts are arranged to celebrate.

Eid al-Fitr

Eid al-Fitr, meaning 'breaking the fast', marks the end of Ramadan. Traditionally people decorate their homes with lights, share gifts, say special prayers and read from the takbirat.

Bastille Day

Bastille Day celebrates the storming of the Bastille in 1789 by the Parisian revolutionaries. It also celebrates the unity of the French people one year later in 1790. Military parades, fireworks and organised gatherings celebrate the day.

August

National Friendship Day

National Friendship Day aims to celebrate the meaning of friendship through the sharing of flowers, cards and gifts. It is also a time to remember those people who may not have many friends, particularly the elderly, and do kind deeds for them.

Janmashtami

Janmashtami is the Hindu celebration of the birth of Lord Krishna. Krishna's birth was to free the Earth from the evilness of demons. Uriadi, the practice of men forming human towers to break a high-hanging pot of curd, take place as part of the celebrations.

Rama Navami

Rama Navami is a Hindu festival which celebrates the birth of the Hindu god Rama to King Dasharatha and Queen Kausalya. Rama is the seventh incarnation of Lord Vishnu. Traditionally stories are read and offerings of flowers and fruits are taken to the temples.

EXAMPLE PLANNING SHEET FOR SEPTEMBER TO AUGUST

Season	Autumn			Winter			Spring			Summer		
Month	September	October	November	December	January	February	March	April	May	June	July	August
National Celebrations	9 World Teddy Bear Day	8 Poetry Day	8 Remembrance Sunday	25 Christmas	1 New Year	9 Shrove Tuesday	1 St David's Day	2 World Autism Day	National Smile Month	19 Father's Day	4–10 National Childhood Obesity Week	7 National Friendship Day
	11 Grandparent's Day	Harvest	9 Nursery Rhyme Week			14 Valentine's Day	3 World Book Day					
			13 Children in Need		25 Tu B'Shevat		6 Mother's Sunday	23 St George's Day		21 Summer Solstice		
			30 St Andrew's Day		29 Bug Busting Day (head lice)		18–21 Red Nose Day					

International Celebrations	14 Rosh Hashanah 24 Eid al-Adha	2 World Smile Day 31 Halloween	5 Bonfire Night 11 Diwali	4–16 Hanukkah	25 Burns' Night	8 Chinese New Year (Monkey)	17 St Patrick's Day 25–28 Easter	15 Rama Navami 22 Passover	15 Buddha Day	6 Ramadan	4 Independence Day 6 Eid al-Fitr 14 Bastille Day Olympics	25 Janmashtami
Possible Activities	Shofar making, cooking	Crafts	Firework exploration, poppy creation	Christmas traditions from around the world	Scottish dancing, Literacy and poems, seed planting	Pancake making, crafts/gifts cards	Gifts, dress-up day, fundraising	Silk Painting, Afikoman bag	Lotus flowers, storytelling, meditation	Standing stones, construction	Henna designs, physical focus/healthy foods	Rangoli patterns, Vishnu crowns, pot making
Outings/Visitors	Teddy bear picnic, last night of the Proms	OAP home	Soldiers/armed forces, visit to memorials, planetarium	Santa/Christmas lights trip	Art museum	China Spirit, Chinatown, fire station, nurse, police	Welsh Mountain Zoo	Garden Centre	Dentist, Pine Forest	Pirate ship and ferry	Sports coaches, local clubs	Transport museum

Season	Autumn			Winter			Spring			Summer		
Month	September	October	November	December	January	February	March	April	May	June	July	August
Math Focus	Olive green and bronze: positional language	Amber and rust: square; size grouping	Navy blue, orange and plum: counting backwards	Scarlet and fern green: more than/less than	Silver, white and marine blue: quantity grouping	Magenta pink and violet: bar charts, tallys	Apple green and crimson red: addition	Lemon and cream: subtraction	Jade and gold: sharing and dividing	Sky blue and ebony: sinking and floating	Turquoise ivory and coral: 3D shapes	Slate grey and terracotta: speed and distance
Literacy Focus	3 Little Pigs	Little Red Hen	3 Green Men of Glen Nevis	T'was The Night Before Christmas	One Snowy Night	Guess How Much I Love You	Owl Babies, St Patrick's Book	George and the Dragon	The Story of Buddha	Peace at Last	Around the World in 80 Days	Rama and Sita
		Room on the Broom	A Diwali Story	The Hanukkah Mouse						Jake and the Neverland Pirates		
New Experiences	Bread making, apple cake, chapatti, spicy rice	Harvest festival collection, party	Shadow puppets, Indian foods	Pantomime, Jewish foods and traditions	Scottish dancing, foods, tree fruits	Lion Dance, Chinese foods	Welsh foods, songs	Archery, panakam	Thai foods, lotus flowers, butterfly hatching	Lantern making	Cultural dance, costumes, French foods	Vishnu crowns, pot making
Possible Focus	All About Me	Autumn/hibernation	Space	Christmas	Winter, transitions	People Who Help Us	Spring, babies	Fairy tales	Bugs	Pirates, transitions	Holidays	Transport

RESOURCES AND FURTHER READING

Channel training

http://course.ncalt.com/Channel_General_Awareness/01/index.html

Department of Education – Prevent Duty

www.gov.uk/government/organisations/ofsted

EAL Support

www.naldic.org.uk

http://uk.mantralingua.com

Early Education

www.early-education.org.uk/development-matters-early-years-foundation-stage-eyfs-download

Equality Act 2010

www.gov.uk/discrimination-your-rights/types-of-discrimination

www.legislation.gov.uk/ukpga/2010/15/contents

Foundation Years

www.foundationyears.org.uk/eyfs-statutory-framework

Ofsted

www.gov.uk/government/organisations/ofsted

www.gov.uk/government/uploads/system/uploads/attachment _data/file/457037/Inspecting_safeguarding_in_early_years_education_and_skills_settings.pdf

www.gov.uk/government/publications/early-years-inspection-handbook-from-september-2015

Pacey – British Values

www.pacey.org.uk/working-in-childcare/spotlight-on/british-values

INDEX